Mystic Caterpillar

Sean Williams

ISBN: 978-0-578-08996-6

MYSTIC CATERPILLAR

In a strangely familiar way, there once was a young caterpillar named Will. Will the caterpillar came to be, (was born) and grew up in a caterpillar town. During caterpillar school, Will always asked plenty of questions, more questions than any of the other caterpillars. One day, his teacher asked him, "why all the questions?" Will answered, "Some of the things you are teaching us don't feel right, and sometimes I get confused." The teacher said, "Don't challenge the knowledge of the ancient ones. Our great leader gathered all this information and put it together so that we may teach the same things to all the generations of caterpillar kind. In this way we may advance our caterpillar society. Will sat and thought for a moment, then asked, "Then why is it so confusing?" The teacher thought for a moment, then answered, "Some things you need to mature in order to understand completely."

After class, Will climbed to the highest branch on the caterpillar school tree, looked around and thought about what his teacher had said about needing to mature. He began to feel confused again when suddenly, one of the female caterpillars joined him at the top of the tree and asked, "What are you doing up here, all by yourself?" Will answered, "Did today's lesson make sense to you?" She answered, "Yeah, why? Did it not make sense to you?" Will answered, "Some parts did, but some did not, to me, it seems like something is missing, or they are not telling us everything they should. It almost feels as though they are hiding something." She asked, "Why concern yourself with such things?" "Why not just learn what they want to teach you and then just use that to go on

1

with your life and be happy like the rest of us?" Will answered, "I cannot stop thinking about it. Something doesn't feel right, it doesn't make sense." She answered, "Well, I came up here to get you to come down and join the rest of us, but obviously we are not important to you, so when you get done thinking, I'll be down there waiting, but don't make me wait too long."

She left and caterpillar watched her go, then turned around and watched as the sun began to set, and thought to himself, "Something doesn't feel right. What am I missing?"

As Will watched, the sun began to dip into the horizon. Will suddenly noticed, the silhouette of another tree, far, far, away, in the distance. As the sun moved behind the tree, Will thought, "I wonder what kind of tree that is?" Suddenly Will thought he saw something move on the tree. He squinted his eyes to see, but just then the sun dipped below the horizon, and as suddenly as the distant tree had appeared, it disappeared. Will thought, "I wonder if anyone else has ever seen that? Maybe my teacher will know of it." Will the caterpillar began his climb down.

The next day at school, during class, Will raised one of his hands. When the teacher asked, "Yes Will, what is it?" Will asked, "Have you ever seen a tree in the distance, just as the sun is beginning to set?" The teacher's mouth hung open as Will's question caught her off guard. She looked around at all the other caterpillars, who were now paying close attention and said, "No, but you shouldn't look into the sun, because you can damage your eyes. Now let's move on." She changed the subject as quickly as possible and continued the lesson. After class she asked Will to remain behind.

After all the other caterpillars had gone, she looked directly at Will and said, "I'm being very serious right now. Stop disrupting class by asking so many questions and by filling your fellow student's heads with legends of distant trees. Many caterpillars have left in pursuit of "the legend of the distant tree" only to never return. Because so many have been lost in that pursuit, the elders have named it "the tree of death." They have done this to discourage any "would-be" adventure "seekers" from setting out in search of it. They have done this to protect our caterpillar society, and have told us to avoid talking about it, and to turn in to them any who do talk of it." They both stood in silence for a moment, then she said, "But I like you Will, so I will not turn you in, but I will ask you one more time, not to speak of it again." Will was about to say something, but he knew she was serious, so he closed his mouth, nodded his head and turned to leave. As he was leaving, she called out behind him, "Thanks for understanding, see you tomorrow in class." As soon as he was out of her sight, he turned and began his climb to the top of the tree.

He got to the top just as the sun had begun to set and looked into the distance again. Just as before, as the sun touched the horizon, a silhouette of a tree appeared. Will thought, "I wonder if I can make it to that tree?" "I wonder why none who have gone in search have ever come back?" As the sun disappeared behind the horizon, the silhouette also disappeared. Will began his climb down to where his friends were. Over the next couple of days Will couldn't stop thinking about that distant tree. He went to look at it every sunset. Not being able to talk about it with his friends or ask any on else about it, was driving him crazy.

The last day of the school week came and again he climbed the tree to watch the sun set, and as it did, the tree shape appeared again, but this time he saw something move, for sure. He was positive of what he had seen. He thought, "I have to go, if I don't, I'm going to go crazy." As the sun disappeared he began his climb back down the tree and thought, "That does it. Tomorrow morning, I'm leaving. I'll find that tree and come back with proof or die trying."

The next morning he set out in the direction of the distant tree. Along the way there were some terrifying experiences, mainly an overactive imagination, because of listening to everyone talk of how dangerous the wilderness was. It took him two full days but he eventually made it.

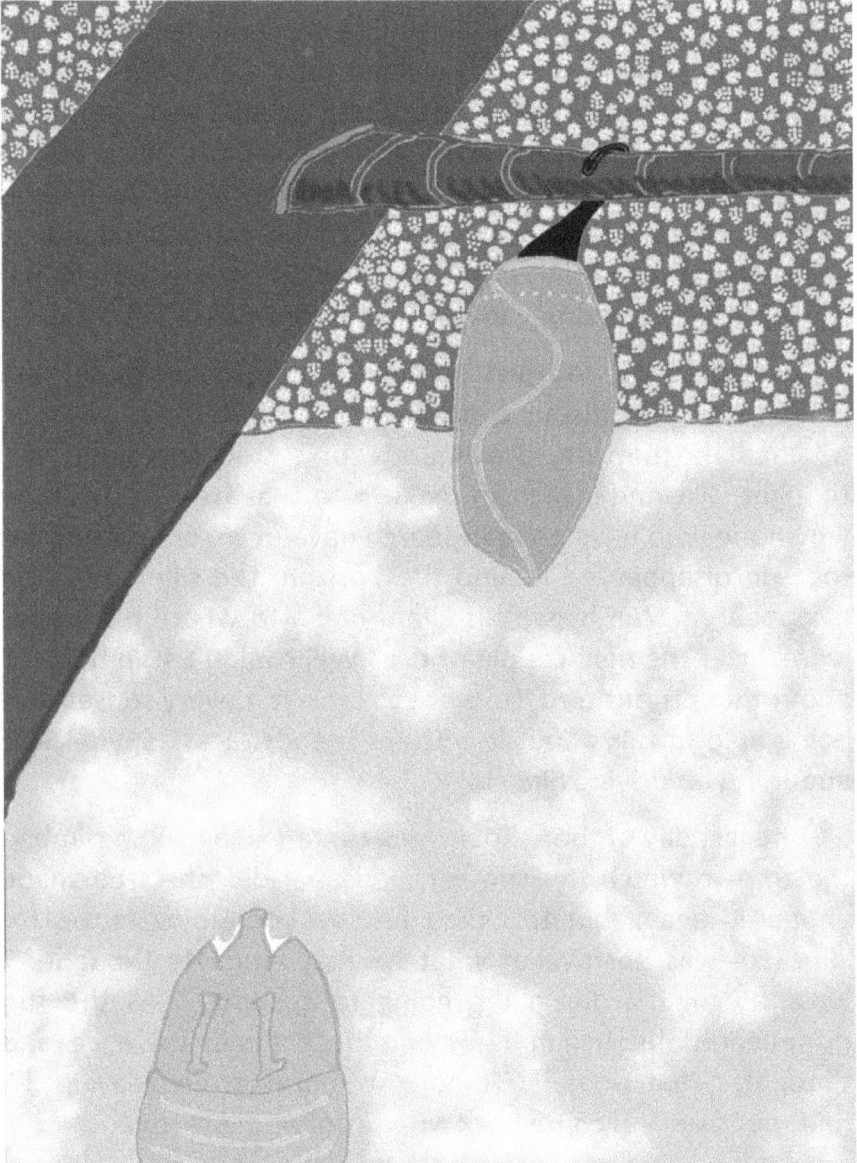

As he approached the tree, he thought, "That wasn't so hard." He saw some strange looking green things hanging from the branches. As he stood there staring, something dropped onto one of the lowest branches from a higher branch and caught his attention.

It was a strange looking creature that was mostly covered by a cape of sorts, with only its head and eyes exposed and they seemed to be looking right at him. Suddenly it spoke! It asked, "Well, what are you waiting for? Aren't you going to climb up and eat?' Will stood there with his mouth open, not knowing what to say. Finally he managed to say, "I've been told it is a tree of death, that it is poisonous." The strange looking creature looked down in amazement and started laughing.

Will got a confused look on his face, as he did not understand why, what he had said, could be regarded as funny. The creature stopped laughing and apologized, then said, "You must have come from the caterpillar society of the west." Again Will looked confused and said, "I came from that direction," and pointed in the direction from where he had come. The creature looked down at Will the caterpillar, smiled and said, "I knew it, because I came from there too, but that was a long time ago." Will asked, "What are you?" "I've never seen anything like you."

The creature smiled again and said, "We are more alike than you can possibly understand in your current condition, but I cannot explain it to you because there is too much that you don't yet know." Will looked at the green things hanging from the branch on which the creature was standing and asked, "What are those things?" The creature looked down at the hanging things and said, "Again, I can't explain it to you in a way that you can understand it right now. All I can say is, at one time they were caterpillars just like you." Will was shocked! He asked, "What happened to them?" "Are they dead?" The creature could tell that Will was becoming frightened and quickly answered, "No, they aren't dead, just changing."

Will stared at them with a puzzled expression until the creature spoke again. "In order for you to find the answers you seek, we must start from the beginning." Will asked, "What beginning?" The creature answered, "Why don't you climb to the top of this tree with me? There's something you need to see." Will agreed and began to climb to the top of the tree following the creature. The creature hopped from branch to branch with Will struggling to keep up.

When they reached the top of the tree, the creature pointed one of its legs in the direction of the caterpillar society of the west. The creature said, "Okay now, notice that you can see no trees like this one anywhere between here and where you came from. Will looked on, agreed, and said, "Yeah, I know. I came here for that very reason." The creature said, "Okay now, turn around and look the other way."

Will turned around and looked. He immediately noticed trees like the one he was in, as far into the distance as he could see. He stared in amazement over the tops of the trees until the creature spoke again. It said, "There once was a time in which these trees spread out in both directions and true knowledge of the purpose of the trees was common, well known, and taught to all. Will looked in both directions again. The creature said, "But then everything changed." Will asked, "What happened?"

The creature paused in thought for a moment, then said, "A great evil came to our world and caused some of the leaders of the caterpillar society to become selfish, greedy, lazy, and power hungry. That lust for power and control caused them to destroy all the trees." Will asked, "But why destroy all the trees." The creature said, "To hide the truth." Will asked, "What truth?"

The creature answered, "You must begin to eat from the tree before you will be capable of fully understanding the answer to that question." Will looked down at the green things hanging from the lower branches and said, "But I don't want to end up like that!" The creature said, "Don't worry, It takes a lot to bring about that kind of change, and when it's your turn, you will welcome it." He paused. "But for now, a few bites will merely begin your journey, of which, the first step is simply a change of mind."

Will looked at the creature, thinking of what he had said, and then asked, "What part should I eat?" The creature looked over to a lower branch which had some strange, light blue, umbrella shaped things sticking out of a ball of white fluff and said, "Begin by eating only one of those umbrella things." Will climbed over to the branch and looked at the umbrella shaped things. He asked, "Are you sure about this?"

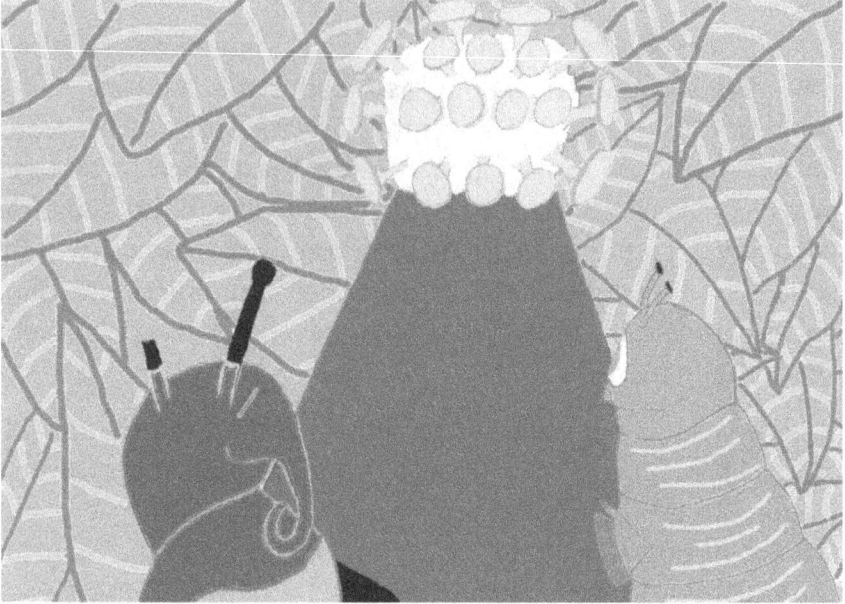

The creature hopped over to where he was, and said, "I can only help you to find the door. It is entirely up to you to choose to walk through." Will got a puzzled look on his face and asked, "What do you mean?" The creature thought for a moment, then answered, "Each and every caterpillar is responsible for making their own choices. That is after all the concept of "free will." This includes choosing to move beyond the limited way of life created by the limited knowledge of the caterpillar society of the west." Will looked in the direction from whence he came.

The creature spoke again, "I will tell you this; once you open that door, it is a door that doesn't close again. Once you know the truth, you cannot UN-know. There is no going back." Will looked at the umbrella shaped things and said, "I don't understand." The creature spoke again. It said, "There is no one that can explain it to you in a way that you would understand, because true knowledge and understanding comes only from and through experience." Will still looked confused, so the creature said, "I've said all I can, and after all, I am not your teacher. You must make your own choice, either eat or don't." After saying that, the creature stood patiently waiting and watching as Will tried to decide what to do.

Will thought for a second, and then said, "I don't know what to do. I'm kind of used to someone else telling me what I should do, you know, telling me what is right." The creature said, "Seems pretty sad going through your whole life, never making your own decisions, but rather just doing what you are told is "right." Will looked at the umbrella things and thought, "My teacher and the rest of them would tell me not to eat, but they also told me that I would die just coming here, which I did not." Will continued thinking. "Hmmn" he thought, "I didn't come all this way for nothing. I guess a little bite won't hurt."

Will stepped forward and pulled on one of the umbrella things, but it wouldn't budge. The creature said, "You need to twist and pull at the same time." With a twist and a pull, Will pulled the umbrella shaped thing out of the white fluff and took a small bite.

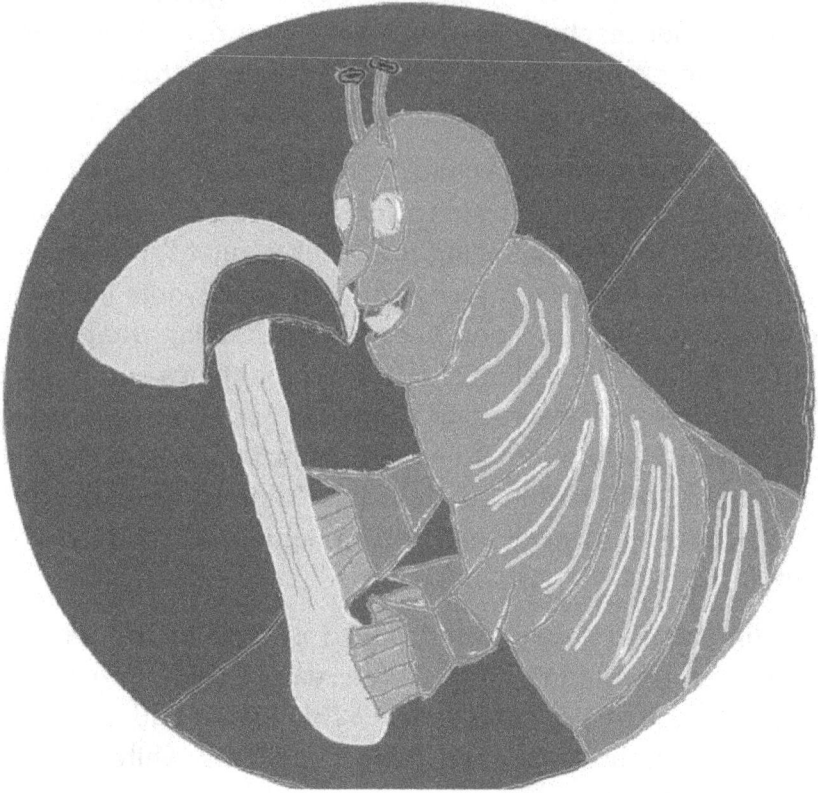

He chewed it up, swallowed and thought, "It tastes a bit like a mixture between grass and a moldy leaf." Then he thought, "But it's actually not that bad." He quickly finished off the rest of the one he had picked, and was about to move for another, when the creature stopped him.

The creature said, "Whoa there, slow down, not too much now!" Will stopped in his tracks and looked up at the creature. He asked, "Okay, now what." The creature replied, "Now...We wait." Will asked, "Wait for what?" The creature said, "Shouldn't be long now." Will was about to ask, "What shouldn't be.... Just as he felt his stomach, tighten and begin to rumble. He looked down at his stomach, but couldn't understand why. Then he suddenly threw his head back, with his eyes wide open looking toward the creature with a terrified look on his face and "oh, no, am I dying?" on his mind.

The creature looked into Will's eyes and watched them dilate and said, "Ok, just relax now and let go." Will relaxed and the creature watched his expression change from one of terror to one of amazement. Waves of knowledge and information flooded Will's mind. It seemed like every question he ever asked or even thought of, he was now suddenly receiving the answers, to all at once. Everything was making perfect sense. The confusion was gone.

All Will kept saying was "Oh, Wow!" and "I understand everything." The creature stayed right by his side but he didn't say anything, he just listened. Will seemed to lose track of time because it seemed like only a few moments since he ate that little umbrella while the sun was just setting. But suddenly it was, now the middle of the night and the full moon was incredibly bright and casting a silver-blue glow onto the tops of clouds which moved across the sky at an incredible pace. As he looked up into the sky with the stars sparkling brightly, he heard himself ask, "Where do we go from here?" A moment later everything went dark and he had a vision or what seemed to be a movie, in his mind.

The whole process of becoming a butterfly seemed to play out before him. As he imagined becoming a butterfly and flying, the brightness of the stars and moon faded, and he again became aware of his surroundings. Wills eyes returned to normal and he looked around, still disoriented and unsure of what to do with the knowledge he now had.

Will looked at the creature standing nearby and said, "I have to go tell the others." The creature said, "Hang on a second, you can't do that." Will looked at him puzzled and asked, "Why?" The creature said, "Think about it, you could not be told. It just doesn't make sense until you see it for yourself." Will said, "Well then I'll just turn all the way into a butterfly and go back and prove it!" The creature said, "Yeah, I tried that." He turned to the side and wiggled the stump, which was the only thing left of that side wing.

Suddenly Will understood why all the trees were missing. He said, "So they destroyed the trees to prevent us from seeing them for who they truly are. By preventing us from knowing the truth, they have made themselves capable of getting us to believe whatever they want us to believe. Since we don't know truth, we fear death, and they use that fear of death as a way to control those who don't know."

The creature said, "Yes, now you got it, they prevent the children of their society from using what was created purposefully for inspiring thought, awareness, connection and understanding. They have done this for one reason: As long as you don't think for yourself, they can think for you, and as long as they are thinking for you, then you are their slaves, playing whatever roles within their society they offer you. Since you have many, many options to choose from when it comes to what you can do for them so that you can earn money so that you can live within the confines of their system, they trick you into thinking you are free, all the while, only free to keep them comfortable, a free source of energy." "They will destroy any who threaten their power and control."

Will asked, "The leaders of the caterpillar society of the west did that to you?" The creature nodded. He said, "I, like you, wanted to tell the others, to free them from the ignorance imposed on them by their parasitic society leaders, but my way didn't work. They have lookouts and captured me before I could reach the city. Indeed, they are probably already awaiting your return, knowing you left in this direction."

Will looked up into the sky and watched as the first beams of sunlight stretched across the sky. Suddenly everything made sense and he said, "I know what to do." The creature smiled and asked, "What's your plan?" Will said, "You said it yourself. I can't simply tell them. They have to see for themselves. So I will take some of those umbrella things back with me and give to them, the gift of "experience," from which true understanding is gained."

The creature said, "Two problems with that plan." "One is, how are you going to get past the guards?" "Remember, they are probably looking for you." "Second, the umbrella things turn into black mush in the sun, and after a few hours after they are picked." "The trip back to the society of the west in caterpillar form is two days, how will you stop that?" Will thought for a moment, and then smiled. The creature asked, "What?"

Will began, "As far as the guards go, I know some secret paths which I've never seen patrolled. These paths take me in along the riverbed, underground briefly, and then up into the back alley behind the school tree." Creature asked, "What about the second problem?" Will thought back... then answered. "Last month in gathering class, I learned about dehydration, or "drying out," to preserve food. Let me see if I still remember." Will remembered, "I need a cool dry place in the shade, with airflow."

He picked all of the umbrella things on the branch he was on and then climbed down to the bottom of the tree. He gathered all of the fresh umbrella things and arranged them neatly in order next to each other at the bottom of the tree in the shade. Will grabbed a nearby leaf and began fanning the little umbrellas. He kept fanning for quite some time. As the little umbrellas dried out, they shriveled up, becoming much smaller, and they changed colors, changing from blue to grey, and they became hard.

Will said, "That should do it," and placed the hardened umbrellas into a basket he had made out of a leaf and a twig. He then placed another leaf over the top and tucked it in, saying, "This should protect them from spoiling in the sun." He pulled down a nearby spider's web, twisted it up, and used it to secure the basket to his back.

Will looked up at the creature and said, "Goodbye my friend, thank you." The creature said, "No. Thank you. It was my one remaining desire to share the unexplainable truth with another. Thank you for letting me take part in your awakening, I now pass the torch of messenger to you. Free them from their ignorance. Show them the way."

Will nodded and turned to leave. He took a few steps and then turned back around to see the creature cast off its cape and two beautiful bright blue wings which looked to be made of pure energy burst out in place of the old torn off ones. The creature turned into a beautiful blue butterfly. He yelled

"Woo-hoo," flew into the sky and did a back flip loop de loop. Will smiled and waved goodbye as his friend flew away.

As Will turned back around and began walking again, he couldn't help but think, "One day I hope to become like that and just fly away without a care or desire in the world, but not yet. I must see this through first. I will see the truth, become known." So he continued on, in the direction of the caterpillar society of the west. Along the way he tried to stay out of sight. He traveled on through a winding valley, along a river and thought, "As long as I stay in this ravine, I should be fine, they never patrol here."

Ironically, as soon as he thought that, he heard something rustle above him and looked up to see a leaf hanging over the ravine with a caterpillar sitting on it. The caterpillar was looking down at him. Will recognized the caterpillar as one of his classmates, named James, and smiled. James asked, "Where have you been?" "We've all been looking for you." Will looked at James and asked, "Why?" James got a puzzled look on his face, as he tried to think of why they had been looking for him.

James answered, "I don't know. I was only told to be on the lookout for you in case you might be in danger, (or "dangerous" as he remembered briefing). There is a rumor going around that you left in search of the forbidden tree of death. Is that true?" Will thought for a second, and then said, "Well yes, I did set out to find the mysterious "Tree of death," but never did. Instead I found something much different, and can tell you truthfully, that my real journey has only just begun."

James instantly got a confused look on his face and Will understood that he could say no more. He watched as James's expression changed from confused to angry. James said, "Well whatever the case, I've been told to take you straight to the guards, if I see you." Will asked, "James, you know me right?" James nodded. Will said, "Then as a friend, let me just go home, let me get something to eat, I'm starving. Then as soon as I'm done eating, I'll turn myself in.

James thought for a moment then said, "Okay, but remember, tomorrow the guards will be knocking on your door." Will smiled and said, "Thank you. I'm going to leave you a present in payment of this favor. Make sure you find your way down to it." James thought, "A present!" and began climbing down. James was so focused on the "present" that he didn't even notice that Will had walked away as he was climbing down. He reached the spot where Will had left the little folded leaf on the rocks. James opened the leaf to find a shriveled up umbrella and thought, "What kind of "present" is this?"

James sniffed the umbrella and then tossed it into his mouth. He chewed it up and thought, "A little crunchy, but not that bad," as he swallowed. After he swallowed he looked around for any that might have dropped, but when he didn't find any, he began walking in the direction that Will had gone. As James walked along he noticed his stomach begin to tighten up on its own. He looked down at the pebbles at his feet. The pebbles seemed to move! On their own! They even seemed to change size right before James' eyes.

He thought, "What is going on?" James looked up into the sky and noticed that darkness began creeping in from all directions. He thought, "Oh, no, what was that thing? I hope I'm not dying!" as the darkness enveloped him. He again thought, "Oh, no!" "I am dying!" but then James became fascinated by a bright light coming closer to him and getting bigger as it came. Suddenly the darkness was gone, and James watched a story play out in his mind. He watched as caterpillars ate the umbrellas and became butterflies. When the movie in his mind faded and he became aware of his "surroundings" again, he thought, "Where's Will?" "I gotta go find Will. I have to know more. At least find out what "that" was, if anything."

As he began walking in the direction of Will's house, he noticed that all of a sudden it seemed to be the middle of the night. James thought, "That's weird, it seems like only moments ago it was early. Yes I'm sure that when I ate that thing, it was only sunset, and now the moon is high in the sky. What is going on?" James asked himself confusedly. James continued on in the direction of Will's house. When James reached Will's house, he noticed quite a few other caterpillars had gathered there already.

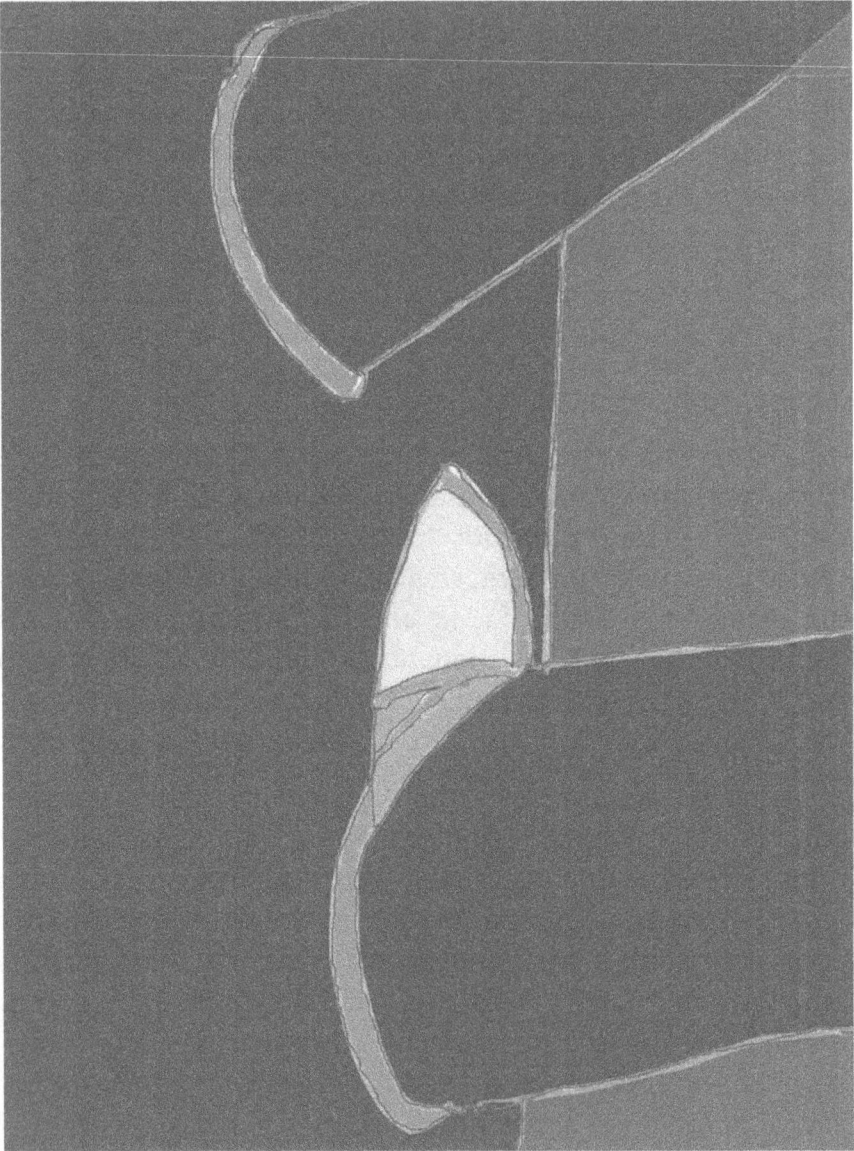

He climbed the tree and walked into Will's open door to find many of his caterpillar friends sitting there with their mouths "Agape" and eyes wide open, pupils fully open, staring into nothing.

James asked, "What's going on here?" Will said "Shhh, be

quiet, don't disturb them." Will took James outside and asked if he had eaten his present. James answered, "Yes." Will asked him about what he had "seen." After James had explained seeing a terrifying darkness, like death, the bright light and the process of becoming butterflies, Will asked, "Did it not make sense to you?" James thought about it again and then said, "yeah, kind of, but what was that, and why did it make me see and experience that?"

Will answered, "What you ate, was what we are all meant to eat, but we have been prevented, by those in control. The small amount that you ate was merely enough to open your mind to the truth, but not enough to make you fully change. It was only enough to show you the way. From here on, you must choose for yourself what direction your life journey takes. You can stay here and work within the confines of this society, eating and doing only what they approve, or you can follow your inner voice and live the life you were meant to live, your true way, either way, the choice is yours."

James thought about that choice for a moment then said, "Thank you Will, for helping me realize the choice, and helping me to realize that I was being prevented from making my own choice by being kept ignorant of the true nature of those things." James fell silent for a moment, and then asked, "Why would they do such a thing and hide the truth like they have done?" Will answered, "You must see them as "Who they are" in order to find the answer to that question." James thought again, and then realized, "By preventing us from seeing the truth, they prevent us from knowing what to do to move on, taking our energy with us. By preventing us from seeing truth clearly, and thereby, making the choice, they've trapped us all and turned us all into energy slaves."

Will smiled, and said, "What you know is a truth that can't be told. The only way share that "light" (knowledge) is through the sharing of experience." James sat thinking for a while, then said, "I understand, thank you for showing me the way." James turned and began climbing down the tree. When he got to the bottom, he set out in the direction of the "tree of death" as it was known. Will watched him go and smiled as he turned to go in to where his other friends were.

As he entered the room, he heard his other friends saying "Oh-wow" as they appeared to look through the ceiling. Will knew they were actually looking inward, and thinking of what they were seeing, thought back and smiled. He found that remembering truth and the moment of change, and his mission to help his friends understand and find truth, brought him an incredible feeling of inner peace and focus on what he had set out do.

After Will's caterpillar friends' visions were over, Will spent the rest of the night and into the early morning hours answering questions and helping them understand, by asking them questions and speaking sayings to them which made them think, using their understanding of truth. Will knew that through the use of their understanding of truth, their understanding is solidified and the connection is made. He helped them by sharing his understandings until he heard a 'knock' on the door.

When one of his friends answered the door, two guards rushed in, pushing his friend to the floor. One of the two guards said, "There he is!" They rushed over and grabbed him. Will looked at them as they pulled him to his feet. One of the guards said, "You're coming with us. The ancient ones want to speak with you." Will said, "I know what you are here for, even though you do not." The guards looked at each other and one said, "Did you hear that?" "He thinks he's better than us," said the other. That guard rushed forward and punched him in the face. As soon as Will's friends saw that, they also rushed forward and began struggling and fighting with the guards. Will stopped his friends and said, "Violence is not the way. Everything is as it should be." The guards led him out of his house.

One of the guards laughed evilly and slapped Will on the back of his head. The guard said, "That's right, you better come with us, if you know what's good for you." Will answered, "I will come although, you do not have any power over me." The guards laughed and one said, "We'll see about that," as they led him away. They led him to the ancient ones chamber and Will saw the leader sitting upon a high throne as they walked in. The guards led Will over in front of the throne and left him standing there.

The ancient leader stood and looked at Will for quite some time. Finally the leader spoke. "I have been told that you went in search of the tree of death." Will replied "That is true, but I found something much different." The leader said, "Explain." Will said, "I found the tree, but it is more a tree of "Life," of "Change," of "Knowledge," and when I ate of it, I realized the truth about the direction my life and indeed, all of our lives, were meant to go."

The leader's mouth opened as if he was about to say something, but just then, one of his advisors approached and whispered, "Quite a few of the younger caterpillars know that he is here, and that he returned from the tree alive. If we make him disappear now, it may become difficult for us." The leader looked down at Will and thought for a moment, and then he said, "For breaking the law, by going off in search of the tree of death, as punishment, you will be banished from our society. You are never to return, as an example to any who would seek to break our laws as you have done."

Will thought of James and the others whom had already eaten of the umbrellas from the tree of change and smiled.

His smile made the leader furious. The leader asked, "Are you not afraid? You will surely die in the wilderness without the comforts of the caterpillar society." Will looked into the ancient one's eyes and said, "I've already sown the seed of truth and seen it take root. There's nothing more that this society can offer me that I need, because I need nothing more than truth, and I already have that within."

Will watched the ancient one's expression change to anger and he said, "Then we'll make an example of you! Guards! Take him to the courtyard and call an assembly!" The guards grabbed him and shoved him towards the door. By the time they got him down to the courtyard, other caterpillars had begun to gather and whisper amongst themselves. Will saw some of his friends who had already eaten of the little umbrellas. He motioned for them to get away from there. Will thought, "Go hide my brothers, I have done all I can for you," as he remembered the creature saying to him.

Quite a few caterpillars had gathered by this time and the ancient one stood up on a branch and announced, "Will caterpillar has broken our law. He has chosen to go against our way, the way of the great caterpillar society, and because of that, we have no choice but to banish him for the rest of his days. So bear witness of him and make sure you follow the rules of our society, so you others don't share his fate." The guards escorted him to the main gate and sent him on his way, closing the gate behind him.

Will looked back at the gate, then began walking in the direction of the sunset and thought, "Well, I've done what I can, I've shown many the truth, and they still have some of those things left, with which to help their friends see the truth, which is ultimately what will set them free. My hope is with them." Will felt happy knowing that he had done what he had set out to do. He heard his inner voice say, "It's time, It's your turn now." He looked up into the sky and smiled as he walked along. Will walked in the direction of the tree; happily knowing that he did all he could for the others.

When he got to the tree, He saw his friend James hanging down from a branch and beginning to form a cocoon. James noticed him approaching and said, "Thanks again brother." Will looked at him, smiled and said, "You're welcome." Will climbed to the top of the tree and looked in the direction of the caterpillar society of the west. Suddenly he noticed something moving through the grass near the base of the tree. Will went down to see what it was.

When he climbed back down, he realized it was some of his friends whom had eaten the umbrella things. Will asked, "What about the others?" If you guys are here, who's going to show the rest the truth?" One of the caterpillars looked up at Will and said, "We've already given out all of those things you brought back with you. Everybody knows that you returned from the tree alive. They know your true story. The truth is coming out and there is nothing that the ancient ones can do about it. They will no longer be able to prevent us with their deceptions."

Will smiled and began to climb back up to the top of the tree. Over the next few days, a steady stream of caterpillars came from the society of the west, in search of the tree, in search of their destiny. When Will realized that he had done what he set out to do, he smiled contently and thought, "Well, I guess I can finally let go. It would seem as though my work is done."

Will climbed over to where some of the umbrella things were, and ate until it felt as if he might burst. With a moan, he hung down from the branch on which he was sitting, and watched as the world around him began to disappear behind a green wall that closed in from all directions. Then suddenly everything went dark and Will saw a bright light. Will felt as if he was moving towards the light, without moving at all. He suddenly heard a voice which sounded very familiar, that he knew was not his own, say, "Thank you, my child, for freeing your brothers and sisters. Thank you for being my messenger, for showing them the way, the truth, and the life."

The light Will saw, grew brighter and brighter, until all the darkness was gone. Will heard the voice again say, "Now it is time for you to feel the freedom of flight. Now fly my child!" Will stretched out in all directions and burst out of his cocoon. Everyone who was now there at the tree, were amazed to see him in his new form. They marveled at the beauty of his wings as he gave them a couple of flaps to get the fluids pumping, and the energies flowing. He then flew up in the air, did a loop-de-loop, and yelled "Woo-Hoo!" as he flew away smiling.

The end....or is it just the beginning? Depends on your perspective I guess...

There dwells within this book, a truth that cannot be told, it must be realized within yourself.

I will tell you this. The plight that faces the "children" of humanity, is very similar to what Will the caterpillar overcame. The darkness we overcome in the world, is the darkness within our own hearts. To overcome "the world" we must overcome selfishness. One cannot overcome "the world" without first "surrendering" (letting go of) all attachment to it. After all, it would have been much "easier" and a lot less work (more comfortable), for Will to just stay within the confines of the "structure" of life in society, going "nowhere" fast, doing nothing of true importance with "his life."

There is a "dormant" hero within each of us, and it is this heroic aspect of our lives that we truly seek to know, although most of us are "born" with no real "awareness" of that, vital life element (see kundalini). This is why it is such a gift and a treasure. It waits forever out of reach, until we seek it. Only the one, who seeks, will find. Only the one who knocks, will it be opened to. In order to grasp it, first we must be willing to let go of everything relating to ourselves for the betterment of everyone else. Enlightenment is not gained for selfish purposes and it cannot be grasped with one hand, it requires everything. The greatest treasure "in the world" cannot "be held." It can only be "beholded." Once we find the pure hero (child of God) within ourselves, then the path of the hero (the Christ) lays out before us, easily seen through the knowledge of truth, but still invisible to those without true knowledge. This is why the true "path" is invisible, and the truth cannot be "told," until one takes a "leap" of faith and suddenly "finds themselves" on the path. Fear clouds the mind and hides the path. Only once on the path, does the path become easy to see…. The "truth" can only be shared through experience (gnosis).

In this "story," full of metaphor, the "umbrella things" serve as a "catalyst" for change, yet they are a metaphor for something that truly exists in the "physical human world" (see entheogen psilocybin). I will tell you this: There always has been and always will be a catalyst for the change for the "children" of humanity as well. Seek and you will find, the treasure in the field. "The heavenly Manna" of "the Bible" (Manna is believed to have been created on the first Friday of existence), is also a metaphor for this. The reason for this is simple; our creator and provider (Our heavenly Father), knows precisely what we need, even though "we may not know ourselves." With that said: I wish you good luck, travelers of the way...

Consider this your "wakeup" call...

Sean Williams

The Gospel of Thomas and the Hymn of the Pearl are also forms of the knowledge contained within this book.

The Hymn of the Pearl tells the story, of a young prince (child of God, a.k.a "you") who is sent from the east into Egypt to retrieve a great pearl (of wisdom) from the dragon who rules the west and guards the pearl. But when the Prince gets to Egypt, the dragon becomes aware of his presence and his goal, and seeks to prevent him from reaching his goal, so the dragon captures the prince and makes him eat the heavy food of the Egyptians, which causes him to fall asleep and forget who he was. Much time passes in the west (world), and the prince begins to believe that he's an Egyptian (human), eating Egyptian food, wearing Egyptian clothes, doing Egyptian (human) things. When his father, the king of the east, hears of his son's capture, he sends him a message, which wakes him up and reminds him of who he was and what he was there for. Once "reminded" he takes off the "clothes of the Egyptians" (physical self, matter), overcomes "the dragon" (worldly desire), captures "the pearl" (achieves enlightenment), and returns to the East (the light, life).

The Gospel of Thomas is also an excellent interpretation of this divine knowledge, but most importantly, it was the knowledge of Jesus uncensored by the men who seek to control religion and the world.

These are the secret sayings that the living Jesus spoke and Didymos Judas Thomas recorded.

1. And he said, "Whoever discovers the interpretation of these sayings will not taste death."

2. Jesus said, "Those who seek should not stop seeking until they find. When they find, they will be disturbed. When they are disturbed, they will marvel, and will reign over all. [And after they have reigned they will rest.]"

3. Jesus said, "If your leaders say to you, 'Look, the (Father's) kingdom is in the sky,' then the birds of the sky will precede you. If they say to you, 'It is in the sea,' then the fish will precede you. Rather, the (Father's) kingdom is within you and it is outside you.

When you know yourselves, then you will be known, and you will understand that you are children of the living Father. But if you do not know yourselves, then you live in poverty, and you are the poverty."

4. Jesus said, "The person old in days won't hesitate to ask a little child seven days old about the place of life, and that person will live.

For many of the first will be last, and will become a single one."

5. Jesus said, "Know what is in front of your face, and what is hidden from you will be disclosed to you.

For there is nothing hidden that will not be revealed. [And there is nothing buried that will not be raised.]"

6. His disciples asked him and said to him, "Do you want us to fast? How should we pray? Should we give to charity? What diet should we observe?"

Jesus said, "Don't lie, and don't do what you hate, because all things are disclosed before heaven. After all, there is nothing hidden that will not be revealed, and there is nothing covered up that will remain undisclosed."

7. Jesus said, "Lucky is the lion that the human will eat, so that the lion becomes human. And foul is the human that the lion will eat, and the lion still will become human."

8. And he said, "The person is like a wise fisherman who cast his net into the sea and drew it up from the sea full of little fish. Among them the wise fisherman discovered a fine

large fish. He threw all the little fish back into the sea, and easily chose the large fish. Anyone here with two good ears had better listen!"

9. Jesus said, "Look, the sower went out, took a handful (of seeds), and scattered (them). Some fell on the road, and the birds came and gathered them. Others fell on rock, and they didn't take root in the soil and didn't produce heads of grain. Others fell on thorns, and they choked the seeds and worms ate them. And others fell on good soil, and it produced a good crop: it yielded sixty per measure and one hundred twenty per measure."

10. Jesus said, "I have cast fire upon the world, and look, I'm guarding it until it blazes."

11. Jesus said, "This heaven will pass away, and the one above it will pass away.

The dead are not alive, and the living will not die. During the days when you ate what is dead, you made it come alive. When you are in the light, what will you do? On the day when you were one, you became two. But when you become two, what will you do?"

12. The disciples said to Jesus, "We know that you are going to leave us. Who will be our leader?"

Jesus said to them, "No matter where you are you are to go to James the Just, for whose sake heaven and earth came into being."

13. Jesus said to his disciples, "Compare me to something and tell me what I am like."

Simon Peter said to him, "You are like a just messenger."

Matthew said to him, "You are like a wise philosopher."

Thomas said to him, "Teacher, my mouth is utterly unable to say what you are like."

Jesus said, "I am not your teacher. Because you have drunk, you have become intoxicated from the bubbling spring that I have tended."

And he took him, and withdrew, and spoke three sayings to him. When Thomas came back to his friends they asked him, "What did Jesus say to you?"

Thomas said to them, "If I tell you one of the sayings he spoke to me, you will pick up rocks and stone me, and fire will come from the rocks and devour you."

14. Jesus said to them, "If you fast, you will bring sin upon yourselves, and if you pray, you will be condemned, and if you give to charity, you will harm your spirits.

When you go into any region and walk about in the countryside, when people take you in, eat what they serve you and heal the sick among them.

After all, what goes into your mouth will not defile you; rather, it's what comes out of your mouth that will defile you."

15. Jesus said, "When you see one who was not born of woman, fall on your faces and worship. That one is your Father."

16. Jesus said, "Perhaps people think that I have come to cast peace upon the world. They do not know that I have come to cast conflicts upon the earth: fire, sword, war.

For there will be five in a house: there'll be three against two and two against three, father against son and son against father, and they will stand alone."

17. Jesus said, "I will give you what no eye has seen, what no ear has heard, what no hand has touched, what has not arisen in the human heart."

18. The disciples said to Jesus, "Tell us, how will our end come?"

Jesus said, "Have you found the beginning, then, that you are looking for the end? You see, the end will be where the beginning is.

Congratulations to the one who stands at the beginning: that one will know the end and will not taste death."

19. Jesus said, "Congratulations to the one who came into being before coming into being.

If you become my disciples and pay attention to my sayings, these stones will serve you.

For there are five trees in Paradise for you; they do not change, summer or winter, and their leaves do not fall. Whoever knows them will not taste death."

20. The disciples said to Jesus, "Tell us what Heaven's kingdom is like."

He said to them, "It's like a mustard seed, the smallest of all seeds, but when it falls on prepared soil, it produces a large plant and becomes a shelter for birds of the sky."

21. Mary said to Jesus, "What are your disciples like?"

He said, "They are like little children living in a field that is not theirs. When the owners of the field come, they will say, 'Give us back our field.' They take off their clothes in front of them in order to give it back to them, and they return their field to them.

For this reason I say, if the owners of a house know that a thief is coming, they will be on guard before the thief arrives and will not let the thief break into their house (their domain) and steal their possessions.

As for you, then, be on guard against the world. Prepare

yourselves with great strength, so the robbers can't find a way to get to you, for the trouble you expect will come.

Let there be among you a person who understands.

When the crop ripened, he came quickly carrying a sickle and harvested it. Anyone here with two good ears had better listen!"

22. Jesus saw some babies nursing. He said to his disciples, "These nursing babies are like those who enter the (Father's) kingdom."

They said to him, "Then shall we enter the (Father's) kingdom as babies?"

Jesus said to them, "When you make the two into one, and when you make the inner like the outer and the outer like the inner, and the upper like the lower, and when you make male and female into a single one, so that the male will not be male nor the female be female, when you make eyes in place of an eye, a hand in place of a hand, a foot in place of a foot, an image in place of an image, then you will enter [the kingdom]."

23. Jesus said, "I shall choose you, one from a thousand and two from ten thousand, and they will stand as a single one."

24. His disciples said, "Show us the place where you are, for we must seek it."

He said to them, "Anyone here with two ears had better listen! There is light within a person of light, and it shines on the whole world. If it does not shine, it is dark."

25. Jesus said, "Love your friends like your own soul, protect them like the pupil of your eye."

26. Jesus said, "You see the sliver in your friend's eye, but

you don't see the timber in your own eye. When you take the timber out of your own eye, then you will see well enough to remove the sliver from your friend's eye."

27. "If you do not fast from the world, you will not find the (Father's) kingdom. If you do not observe the sabbath as a sabbath you will not see the Father."

28. Jesus said, "I took my stand in the midst of the world, and in flesh I appeared to them. I found them all drunk, and I did not find any of them thirsty. My soul ached for the children of humanity, because they are blind in their hearts and do not see, for they came into the world empty, and they also seek to depart from the world empty.

But meanwhile they are drunk. When they shake off their wine, then they will change their ways."

29. Jesus said, "If the flesh came into being because of spirit, that is a marvel, but if spirit came into being because of the body, that is a marvel of marvels.

Yet I marvel at how this great wealth has come to dwell in this poverty."

30. Jesus said, "Where there are three deities, they are divine. Where there are two or one, I am with that one."

31. Jesus said, "No prophet is welcome on his home turf; doctors don't cure those who know them."

32. Jesus said, "A city built on a high hill and fortified cannot fall, nor can it be hidden."

33. Jesus said, "What you will hear in your ear, in the other ear proclaim from your rooftops.

After all, no one lights a lamp and puts it under a basket, nor does one put it in a hidden place. Rather, one puts it on a lampstand so that all who come and go will see its light."

34. Jesus said, "If a blind person leads a blind person, both of them will fall into a hole."

35. Jesus said, "One can't enter a strong person's house and take it by force without tying his hands. Then one can loot his house."

36. Jesus said, "Do not fret, from morning to evening and from evening to morning, [about your food--what you're going to eat, or about your clothing--] what you are going to wear. [You're much better than the lilies, which neither card nor spin.

As for you, when you have no garment, what will you put on? Who might add to your stature? That very one will give you your garment.]"

37. His disciples said, "When will you appear to us, and when will we see you?"

Jesus said, "When you strip without being ashamed, and you take your clothes and put them under your feet like little children and trample then, then [you] will see the son of the living one and you will not be afraid."

38. Jesus said, "Often you have desired to hear these sayings that I am speaking to you, and you have no one else from whom to hear them. There will be days when you will seek me and you will not find me."

39. Jesus said, "The Pharisees and the scholars have taken the keys of knowledge and have hidden them. They have not entered nor have they allowed those who want to enter to do so.

As for you, be as sly as snakes and as simple as doves."

40. Jesus said, "A grapevine has been planted apart from the Father. Since it is not strong, it will be pulled up by its root and will perish."

41. Jesus said, "Whoever has something in hand will be given more, and whoever has nothing will be deprived of even the little they have."

42. Jesus said, "Be passersby."

43. His disciples said to him, "Who are you to say these things to us?"

"You don't understand who I am from what I say to you.

Rather, you have become like the Judeans, for they love the tree but hate its fruit, or they love the fruit but hate the tree."

44. Jesus said, "Whoever blasphemes against the Father will be forgiven, and whoever blasphemes against the son will be forgiven, but whoever blasphemes against the holy spirit will not be forgiven, either on earth or in heaven."

45. Jesus said, "Grapes are not harvested from thorn trees, nor are figs gathered from thistles, for they yield no fruit.

Good persons produce good from what they've stored up; bad persons produce evil from the wickedness they've stored up in their hearts, and say evil things. For from the overflow of the heart they produce evil."

46. Jesus said, "From Adam to John the Baptist, among those born of women, no one is so much greater than John the Baptist that his eyes should not be averted.

But I have said that whoever among you becomes a child will recognize the (Father's) kingdom and will become greater than John."

47. Jesus said, "A person cannot mount two horses or bend two bows.

And a slave cannot serve two masters, otherwise that slave will honor the one and offend the other.

Nobody drinks aged wine and immediately wants to drink young wine. Young wine is not poured into old wineskins, or they might break, and aged wine is not poured into a new wineskin, or it might spoil.

An old patch is not sewn onto a new garment, since it would create a tear."

48. Jesus said, "If two make peace with each other in a single house, they will say to the mountain, 'Move from here!' and it will move."

49. Jesus said, "Congratulations to those who are alone and chosen, for you will find the kingdom. For you have come from it, and you will return there again."

50. Jesus said, "If they say to you, 'Where have you come from?' say to them, 'We have come from the light, from the place where the light came into being by itself, established [itself], and appeared in their image.'

If they say to you, 'Is it you?' say, 'We are its children, and we are the chosen of the living Father.'

If they ask you, 'What is the evidence of your Father in you?' say to them, 'It is motion and rest.'"

51. His disciples said to him, "When will the rest for the dead take place, and when will the new world come?"

He said to them, "What you are looking forward to has come, but you don't know it."

52. His disciples said to him, "Twenty-four prophets have spoken in Israel, and they all spoke of you."

He said to them, "You have disregarded the living one who is in your presence, and have spoken of the dead."

53. His disciples said to him, "Is circumcision useful or not?"

He said to them, "If it were useful, their father would produce children already circumcised from their mother. Rather, the true circumcision in spirit has become profitable in every respect."

54. Jesus said, "Congratulations to the poor, for to you belongs Heaven's kingdom."

55. Jesus said, "Whoever does not hate father and mother cannot be my disciple, and whoever does not hate brothers and sisters, and carry the cross as I do, will not be worthy of me."

56. Jesus said, "Whoever has come to know the world has discovered a carcass, and whoever has discovered a carcass, of that person the world is not worthy."

57 Jesus said, "The Father's kingdom is like a person who has [good] seed. His enemy came during the night and sowed weeds among the good seed. The person did not let the workers pull up the weeds, but said to them, 'No, otherwise you might go to pull up the weeds and pull up the wheat along with them.' For on the day of the harvest the weeds will be conspicuous, and will be pulled up and burned."

58. Jesus said, "Congratulations to the person who has toiled and has found life."

59. Jesus said, "Look to the living one as long as you live, otherwise you might die and then try to see the living one, and you will be unable to see."

60. He saw a Samaritan carrying a lamb and going to Judea. He said to his disciples, "that person ... around the lamb." They said to him, "So that he may kill it and eat it." He said to them, "He will not eat it while it is alive, but only after he has killed it and it has become a carcass."

They said, "Otherwise he can't do it."

He said to them, "So also with you, seek for yourselves a place for rest, or you might become a carcass and be eaten."

61. Jesus said, "Two will recline on a couch; one will die, one will live."

Salome said, "Who are you mister? You have climbed onto my couch and eaten from my table as if you are from someone."

Jesus said to her, "I am the one who comes from what is whole. I was granted from the things of my Father."

"I am your disciple."

"For this reason I say, if one is whole, one will be filled with light, but if one is divided, one will be filled with darkness."

62. Jesus said, "I disclose my mysteries to those [who are worthy] of [my] mysteries.

63 Jesus said, "There was a rich person who had a great deal of money. He said, 'I shall invest my money so that I may sow, reap, plant, and fill my storehouses with produce, that I may lack nothing.' These were the things he was thinking in his heart, but that very night he died. Anyone here with two ears had better listen!"

64. Jesus said, "A person was receiving guests. When he had prepared the dinner, he sent his slave to invite the guests.

The slave went to the first and said to that one, 'My master invites you.' That one said, 'Some merchants owe me money; they are coming to me tonight. I have to go and give them instructions. Please excuse me from dinner.'

The slave went to another and said to that one, 'My master has invited you.' That one said to the slave, 'I have bought a house, and I have been called away for a day. I shall have no time.'

The slave went to another and said to that one, 'My master invites you.' That one said to the slave, 'My friend is to be married, and I am to arrange the banquet. I shall not be able to come. Please excuse me from dinner.'

The slave went to another and said to that one, 'My master invites you.' That one said to the slave, 'I have bought an estate, and I am going to collect the rent. I shall not be able to come. Please excuse me.'

The slave returned and said to his master, 'Those whom you invited to dinner have asked to be excused.' The master said to his slave, 'Go out on the streets and bring back whomever you find to have dinner.'

Buyers and merchants [will] not enter the places of my Father."

65. He said, "A [...] person owned a vineyard and rented it to some farmers, so they could work it and he could collect its crop from them. He sent his slave so the farmers would give him the vineyard's crop. They grabbed him, beat him, and almost killed him, and the slave returned and told his master. His master said, 'Perhaps he didn't know them.' He sent another slave, and the farmers beat that one as well. Then the master sent his son and said, 'Perhaps they'll show my son some respect.' Because the farmers knew that he was the heir to the vineyard, they grabbed him and killed him. Anyone here with two ears had better listen!"

66. Jesus said, "Show me the stone that the builders rejected: that is the keystone."

67. Jesus said, "Those who know all, but are lacking in themselves, are utterly lacking."

68. Jesus said, "Congratulations to you when you are hated and persecuted; and no place will be found, wherever you have been persecuted."

69. Jesus said, "Congratulations to those who have been persecuted in their hearts: they are the ones who have truly come to know the Father.

Congratulations to those who go hungry, so the stomach of the one in want may be filled."

70. Jesus said, "If you bring forth what is within you, what you have will save you. If you do not have that within you, what you do not have within you [will] kill you."

71. Jesus said, "I will destroy [this] house, and no one will be able to build it [...]."

72. A [person said] to him, "Tell my brothers to divide my father's possessions with me."

He said to the person, "Mister, who made me a divider?"

He turned to his disciples and said to them, "I'm not a divider, am I?"

73. Jesus said, "The crop is huge but the workers are few, so beg the harvest boss to dispatch workers to the fields."

74. He said, "Lord, there are many around the drinking trough, but there is nothing in the well."

75. Jesus said, "There are many standing at the door, but those who are alone will enter the bridal suite."

76. Jesus said, "The Father's kingdom is like a merchant who had a supply of merchandise and found a pearl. That merchant was prudent; he sold the merchandise and bought the single pearl for himself.

So also with you, seek his treasure that is unfailing, that is enduring, where no moth comes to eat and no worm destroys."

77. Jesus said, "I am the light that is over all things. I am all:

from me all came forth, and to me all attained.

Split a piece of wood; I am there.

Lift up the stone, and you will find me there."

78. Jesus said, "Why have you come out to the countryside? To see a reed shaken by the wind? And to see a person dressed in soft clothes, [like your] rulers and your powerful ones? They are dressed in soft clothes, and they cannot understand truth."

79. A woman in the crowd said to him, "Lucky are the womb that bore you and the breasts that fed you."

He said to [her], "Lucky are those who have heard the word of the Father and have truly kept it. For there will be days when you will say, 'Lucky are the womb that has not conceived and the breasts that have not given milk.'"

80. Jesus said, "Whoever has come to know the world has discovered the body, and whoever has discovered the body, of that one the world is not worthy."

81. Jesus said, "Let one who has become wealthy reign, and let one who has power renounce <it>."

82. Jesus said, "Whoever is near me is near the fire, and whoever is far from me is far from the (Father's) kingdom."

83. Jesus said, "Images are visible to people, but the light within them is hidden in the image of the Father's light. He will be disclosed, but his image is hidden by his light."

84. Jesus said, "When you see your likeness, you are happy. But when you see your images that came into being before you and that neither die nor become visible, how much you will have to bear!"

85. Jesus said, "Adam came from great power and great wealth, but he was not worthy of you. For had he been

worthy, [he would] not [have tasted] death."

86. Jesus said, "[Foxes have] their dens and birds have their nests, but human beings have no place to lay down and rest."

87. Jesus said, "How miserable is the body that depends on a body, and how miserable is the soul that depends on these two."

88. Jesus said, "The messengers and the prophets will come to you and give you what belongs to you. You, in turn, give them what you have, and say to yourselves, 'When will they come and take what belongs to them?'"

89. Jesus said, "Why do you wash the outside of the cup? Don't you understand that the one who made the inside is also the one who made the outside?"

90. Jesus said, "Come to me, for my yoke is comfortable and my lordship is gentle, and you will find rest for yourselves."

91. They said to him, "Tell us who you are so that we may believe in you."

He said to them, "You examine the face of heaven and earth, but you have not come to know the one who is in your presence, and you do not know how to examine the present moment."

92. Jesus said, "Seek and you will find.

In the past, however, I did not tell you the things about which you asked me then. Now I am willing to tell them, but you are not seeking them."

93. "Don't give what is holy to dogs, for they might throw them upon the manure pile. Don't throw pearls [to] pigs, or they might ... it [...]."

94. Jesus [said], "One who seeks will find, and for [one who knocks] it will be opened."

95. [Jesus said], "If you have money, don't lend it at interest. Rather, give [it] to someone from whom you won't get it back."

96. Jesus [said], "The Father's kingdom is like [a] woman. She took a little leaven, [hid] it in dough, and made it into large loaves of bread. Anyone here with two ears had better listen!"

97. Jesus said, "The [Father's] kingdom is like a woman who was carrying a [jar] full of meal. While she was walking along [a] distant road, the handle of the jar broke and the meal spilled behind her [along] the road. She didn't know it; she hadn't noticed a problem. When she reached her house, she put the jar down and discovered that it was empty."

98. Jesus said, "The Father's kingdom is like a person who wanted to kill someone powerful. While still at home he drew his sword and thrust it into the wall to find out whether his hand would go in. Then he killed the powerful one."

99. The disciples said to him, "Your brothers and your mother are standing outside."

He said to them, "Those here who do what my Father wants are my brothers and my mother. They are the ones who will enter my Father's kingdom."

100. They showed Jesus a gold coin and said to him, "The Roman emperor's people demand taxes from us."

He said to them, "Give the emperor what belongs to the emperor, give God what belongs to God, and give me what is mine."

101. "Whoever does not hate [father] and mother as I do cannot be my [disciple], and whoever does [not] love [father

and] mother as I do cannot be my [disciple]. For my mother [...], but my true [mother] gave me life."

102. Jesus said, "Damn the Pharisees! They are like a dog sleeping in the cattle manger: the dog neither eats nor [lets] the cattle eat."

103. Jesus said, "Congratulations to those who know where the rebels are going to attack. [They] can get going, collect their imperial resources, and be prepared before the rebels arrive."

104. They said to Jesus, "Come, let us pray today, and let us fast."

Jesus said, "What sin have I committed, or how have I been undone? Rather, when the groom leaves the bridal suite, then let people fast and pray."

105. Jesus said, "Whoever knows the father and the mother will be called the child of a whore."

106. Jesus said, "When you make the two into one, you will become children of Adam, and when you say, 'Mountain, move from here!' it will move."

107. Jesus said, "The (Father's) kingdom is like a shepherd who had a hundred sheep. One of them, the largest, went astray. He left the ninety-nine and looked for the one until he found it. After he had toiled, he said to the sheep, 'I love you more than the ninety-nine.'"

108. Jesus said, "Whoever drinks from my mouth will become like me; I myself shall become that person, and the hidden things will be revealed to him."

109. Jesus said, "The (Father's) kingdom is like a person who had a treasure hidden in his field but did not know it. And [when] he died he left it to his [son]. The son [did] not know about it either. He took over the field and sold it. The buyer

went plowing, [discovered] the treasure, and began to lend money at interest to whomever he wished."

110. Jesus said, "Let one who has found the world, and has become wealthy, renounce the world."

111. Jesus said, "The heavens and the earth will roll up in your presence, and whoever is living from the living one will not see death."

Does not Jesus say, "Those who have found themselves, of them the world is not worthy"?

112. Jesus said, "Damn the flesh that depends on the soul. Damn the soul that depends on the flesh."

113. His disciples said to him, "When will the kingdom come?"

"It will not come by watching for it. It will not be said, 'Look, here!' or 'Look, there!' Rather, the Father's kingdom is spread out upon the earth, and people don't see it."

[Saying probably added to the original collection at a later date:]

114. Simon Peter said to them, "Make Mary leave us, for females don't deserve life."

Jesus said, "Look, I will guide her to make her male, so that she too may become a living spirit resembling you males. For every female who makes herself male will enter the kingdom of Heaven."

I have created this book for the highest purpose, may it serve you well...

By the "instrument" known as: Sean Williams

www.ingramcontent.com/pod-product-compliance
Lightning Source LLC
Chambersburg PA
CBHW031529040426
42445CB00009B/457